W9-BIA-730

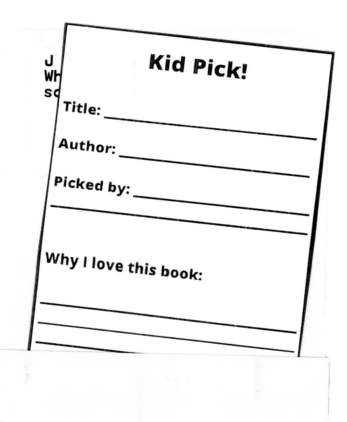

Kid Pick!

Title: _____

Author: _____

Picked by: _____

_____

Why I love this book:

_____

_____

_____

Why Why Why are there schools in the sea?

MC
PUBLISHERS

First published as hardback in 2006 by
Miles Kelly Publishing Ltd, Bardfield Centre,
Great Bardfield, Essex, CM7 4SLCopyright
© Miles Kelly Publishing Ltd 2006

This 2009 edition published and distributed
by:

Mason Crest Publishers Inc.
370 Reed Road, Broomall, Pennsylvania
19008
(866) MCP-BOOK (toll free)
www.masoncrest.com

Why Why Why—
Are There Schools in the Sea?
ISBN 978-1-4222-1572-2
Library of Congress Cataloging-in-
Publication data is available

Why Why Why—?
Complete 23 Title Series
ISBN 978-1-4222-1568-5

Printed in the United States of America

Contents

Is there only one big ocean?

It seems that way. All the oceans flow into each other, but we know them as four different oceans — the Pacific, Atlantic, Indian, and Arctic. The land we live on, the continents, rises out of the oceans. More than two-thirds of the Earth's rocky surface is covered by oceans.

Key

1 Arctic Ocean
2 Atlantic Ocean
3 Pacific Ocean
4 Indian Ocean

Seamount

Plain

Trench

Are there mountains under the sea?

Yes there are. The land beneath the sea is covered by mountains, flat areas called plains and deep valleys called trenches. There are also huge underwater volcanoes called seamounts.

Salty or fresh!

Almost all of the world's water is in the oceans. Only a tiny amount is in freshwater lakes and rivers.

Were do islands come from?

Islands are 'born' beneath the sea. If an underwater volcano erupts, it throws out hot, sticky lava. This cools and hardens in the water. Layers of lava build up and up, until a new island peeps above the waves.

Look

Look at the world map to find where you live. Which ocean is nearest to you?

Do seashells have feet?

Tiny animals called limpets live inside some seashells.
They stick to rocks at the shoreline where they eat slimy, green plants called algae. When the tide is out, limpets stick to the rocks like glue, with a strong muscular foot. They only move when the tide crashes in.

Limpets

Can starfish grow arms?

Yes they can. Starfish may have as many as 40 arms, called rays. If a hungry crab grabs hold of one, the starfish abandons its arm, and uses the others to make its getaway. It then begins to grow a new arm.

Anemone

Starfish

6

Fighting fit!

Anemones are a kind of sea–living plant. Some anemones fight over their feeding grounds. Beadlet anemones shoot sharp, tiny hooks at each other until the weakest one gives in.

When is a sponge like an animal?

Sponges are animals! They are very simple creatures that filter food from sea water. The natural sponge that you use in the bath is a long-dead dried-out sponge!

Crab

Sponge

Find

When you next visit a beach, try to find a rock pool. Write a list of what you see.

Are there schools in the sea?

Some fish live in big groups called schools. This may protect them from hungry hunters. There are thousands of different types of fish in the sea. Most are covered in shiny scales and use fins and tails to swim. Fish have gills that take in oxygen from the water so that they can breathe.

Read

What is a big group of fish called? Read this page to find out.

8

Which fish looks like an oar?

The oarfish does — and it can grow to be as long as four canoes! It is the longest bony fish and is found in all the world's oceans. Oarfish have a bright red fin along the length of their back. They swim upright through the water.

Oarfish

Flying high!

Flying fish cannot really fly. Fish can't survive out of water, but flying fish sometimes leap above the waves when they are swimming at high speed. They use their long fins to glide through the air for as long as 30 seconds.

Do fish like to sunbathe?

Sunfish like sunbathing. Ocean sunfish are huge fish that can weigh as much as one tonne — as heavy as a small car! They like to swim at the surface of the water, as if they're sunbathing.

School of fish

What is the scariest shark?

Great whites are the scariest sharks.
These huge fish speed through the
water at almost 20 miles per
hour. Unlike most fish, the
great white shark has warm blood. This allows
its muscles to work well but it also means that
it needs to eat lots of meat. Great white
sharks are fierce hunters. They will
attack and eat almost anything, but
prefer to feed on seals.

Great white shark

Draw

Using felt-tip
pens, draw your
own underwater
picture. Include a
great white shark.

Do some sharks use hammers?

Not really! Hammerhead sharks have hammer-shaped heads to search for food. With a nostril and an eye on each end of the 'hammer', they swing their heads from side to side, looking for a meal.

Hammerhead shark

Yum yum!

Most sharks are meat eaters. Herring are a favorite food for sand tiger and thresher sharks, while a hungry tiger shark will gobble up just about anything!

When is a shark like a pup?

When it's a baby. Young sharks are called pups. Some grow inside their mother's body. Others hatch from eggs straight into the sea.

Who builds walls beneath the sea?

Tiny animals build underwater walls. These walls are made of coral, the leftover skeletons of tiny sea animals called polyps. Over millions of years, enough skeletons pile up to form walls. These make a coral reef. All kinds of creatures live around a reef.

Parrot fish

Seahorse

Clownfish

Look

Do you know where the Great Barrier Reef is? Look in an atlas to find out.

How do fish keep clean?

Cleaner wrasse are little fish that help other fish to keep clean! Larger fish, such as groupers and moray eels, visit the cleaner wrasse, which nibbles all the bugs and bits of dirt off the bigger fishes' bodies – what a feast!

Coral reef

Super reef

You can see the Great Barrier Reef from space! At 1,300 miles long, it is the largest thing ever built by living creatures.

Lionfish

Cleaner wrasse fish

When is a fish like a clown?

When it's a clownfish. These fish are brightly coloured, like circus clowns. They live among the stinging arms (tentacles) of the sea anemone. Clownfish swim among the stingers, where they are safe from enemies.

Sea anemone

What is the biggest sea animal?

The blue whale is the biggest animal in the ocean – and the whole planet. It is about 100 feet long and can weigh up to 150 tons. It feeds on tiny, shrimp-like creatures called krill – and eats about 4 tons every day! Like other great whales, the blue whale has special, sieve-like parts in its mouth that are called baleen plates.

Blue whale

Can whales sing songs?

All whales make sounds, such as squeaks and moans. The humpback whale really does seem to sing. The males probably do this to attract a mate. He may repeat his song for up to 20 hours!

Humpback whale

Stick around!

Barnacles are shellfish. They attach themselves to ships, or the bodies of grey whales and other large sea animals.

Do whales grow tusks?

The narwhal has a tusk like a unicorn's. This tusk is a long, twirly tooth that comes out of the whale's head. The males use their tusks as weapons when they fight over females. The tusk can grow to 10 feet in length.

Measure

The blue whale is 100 feet long. Can you measure how long you are?

Do lions live in the sea?

There are lions in the sea, but not the furry, roaring kind. Sea lions, seals and walruses are all warm-blooded animals that have adapted to ocean life. They have flippers instead of legs — far more useful for swimming. A thick layer of fat under the skin keeps them warm in cold water.

Think

What do you think whales, dolphins and seals have in common with humans?

Seal

16

Who sleeps in seaweed?

Sea otters do! They live in forests of giant seaweed, called kelp. When they sleep, they wrap strands of kelp around their bodies to stop themselves being washed out to sea.

Sea otter

Sea lion

Singing seal!

Leopard seals sing in their sleep! These seals, found in the Antarctic, chirp and whistle while they snooze.

Can a walrus change color?

Walruses seem to change color. In cold water, a walrus can look pale brown or even white. This is because blood drains from the skin to stop the body losing heat. On land, blood returns to the skin and the walrus looks pink!

Are there crocodiles in the sea?

Most crocodiles live in rivers and swamps. The saltwater crocodile also swims out to sea – it doesn't seem to mind the salty water. These crocodiles are huge, and can grow to be 23 feet long and one ton in weight.

Saltwater crocodile

Find out

Turtles only come ashore for one reason. Can you find out why?

Which lizard loves to swim?

Most lizards live on land, where it is easier to warm up their cold-blooded bodies. Marine iguanas depend on the sea for food. They dive underwater to eat seaweed growing on rocks. When they are not diving, they sit on rocks and soak up the sunshine.

How deep can a turtle dive?

Leatherback turtles can dive up to 4,000 feet for their dinner. They are the biggest sea turtles and they make the deepest dives. Leatherbacks feed mostly on jellyfish but also eat crabs, lobsters and starfish.

Leatherback turtle

Slithery snakes!

There are poisonous snakes in the sea. The banded sea snake and the yellow-bellied sea snake both use poison to kill their prey. Their poison is far stronger than that of land snakes.

Can seabirds sleep as they fly?

Wandering albatrosses are the biggest seabirds and spend months at sea. They are such good gliders that they even sleep as they fly. To feed, they sit on the surface of the water, where they catch creatures such as squid. An albatross has a wingspan of around 10 feet — about the length of a family car!

Wandering albatross

Think

Sea birds have webbed feet. Why do you think this is? Do you have webbed feet?

Do seabirds dig burrows?

Most seabirds make nests on cliffs. The puffin digs a burrow on the clifftop, like a rabbit. Sometimes, a puffin even takes over an empty rabbit hole. Here it lays its egg. Both parents look after the chick when it hatches.

Puffins

Dancing birds!

Boobies are a type of seabird that live in large groups. The males have bright red or blue feet. When they are looking for a mate, they dance in front of the female, trying to attract her with their colourful feet!

Which bird dives for its dinner?

The gannet dives headfirst into the ocean to catch fish in its beak. It dives at high-speed and hits the water hard. Luckily, the gannet is protected by cushions of air inside its head that absorb most of the shock.

How do polar bears learn to swim?

Polar bears are good swimmers and they live around the freezing Arctic Ocean. They learn to swim when they are cubs, by following their mother into the water. With their big front paws, the bears paddle through the water. They can swim for many hours.

Polar bears

Imagine
Pretend to be a penguin. Imagine what life is like at the South Pole.

Are penguins fast swimmers?

Penguins are birds — but they cannot fly. All penguins are fast swimmers. The fastest swimmer is the gentoo penguin. It can reach speeds of 17 miles per hour underwater.

Gentoo penguin

Small and tall!

The smallest penguin is the fairy penguin at just 16 inches tall. The biggest is the emperor penguin at just over 4 feet in height — as tall as a seven-year-old child!

Which penguin dad likes to babysit?

Emperor penguin dads look after the baby chicks. The female lays an egg and leaves her mate to keep it warm. The penguin dad balances the egg on his feet to keep it off the freezing ice. He goes without food until the chick hatches. When it does, the mother returns and both parents look after it.

Is seaweed good to eat?

Seaweed can be very good to eat. In shallow, warm seawater, people can grow their own seaweed. It is then dried in the sun, which helps to keep it fresh. Seaweed is even used to make ice cream!

Growing seaweed

List

Make a list of the things you can eat that come from the ocean. Which of these things have you eaten before?

24

How do we get salt from the sea?

Sea water is salty. Salt is an important substance. In hot, low-lying areas, people build walls to hold shallow pools of sea water. The water dries up in the sun, leaving behind crystals of salt.

How are lobsters caught?

Lobsters are large shellfish that are good to eat. Fishermen catch them in wooden cages called pots. The lobsters are attracted to dead fish placed in the pots. They push the door of the pot open to get to the fish, but once inside, the lobster can't get out again.

Lobster pot

Do pearls grow at sea?

Yes they do. Pearls grow inside oysters, a kind of shellfish. If a grain of sand gets stuck in an oyster's shell, it irritates its soft body. The oyster coats the grain with a substance that it uses to line the inside of its shell. In time, more coats are added and a pearl begins to form.

Are there chimneys under the sea?

Rocky chimneys on the ocean floor give off clouds of hot water. These chimneys lie deep beneath the ocean. The hot water feeds strange creatures such as tube worms and sea spiders.

Rat tail fish

Watery village!

In 1963, diver Jacques Cousteau built a village on the bed of the Red Sea. Along with four other divers, he lived there for a whole month.

Giant clams

Do monsters live in the sea?

Sea monsters do not exist. Long ago, people thought they did. The giant squid may have been mistaken for a monster. It has long arms called tentacles, and eyes as big as dinner plates.

Giant squid

Chimney

What is a mermaid?

Mermaids are strange creatures with the body of a woman and a long fishy tail — but they aren't real. People once thought they lived in the sea and confused sailors with their beautiful singing.

Sea spider

Tube worms

Write

Can you think of any stories or films about mermaids? See if you can write your own underwater mermaid story.

How do divers breathe underwater?

Divers have a spare pair of lungs. Scuba divers carry a special piece of breathing equipment called an 'aqua lung'. These are tanks filled with oxygen (air) that sit on the divers' backs. A long tube supplies the diver with air.

Water record!

A single boat towed 100 waterskiers! This record was made off the coast of Australia in 1986 and no one has beaten it yet. The drag boat was a cruiser called 'Reef Cat'.

Can people ride the waves?

Yes they can, on surfboards. Surfing became popular in the 1950s. Modern surfboards are made of super-light material. People stand up on their boards and ride the waves. The best places to surf are off the coasts of Mexico and Hawaii.

Surfer

Aqua lung

Diver

Wear
Try wearing some goggles in the bath. What can you see?

What is a jet ski?

A jet ski is like a motorbike without wheels that travels on water. It pushes out a jet of water behind it, which pushes it forward. Jet skiers can reach speeds of over 60 miles per hour.

Quiz time

page 9

Do you remember what you have read about oceans? Here are some questions to test your memory. The pictures will help you. If you get stuck, read the pages again.

3. Which fish looks like an oar?

4. Do some sharks use hammers?

page 11

1. Are there mountains under the sea?

page 11

page 5

5. When is a shark like a pup?

2. When is a sponge like an animal?

page 7

page 17

6. Who sleeps in seaweed?

7. Are there crocodiles in the sea?

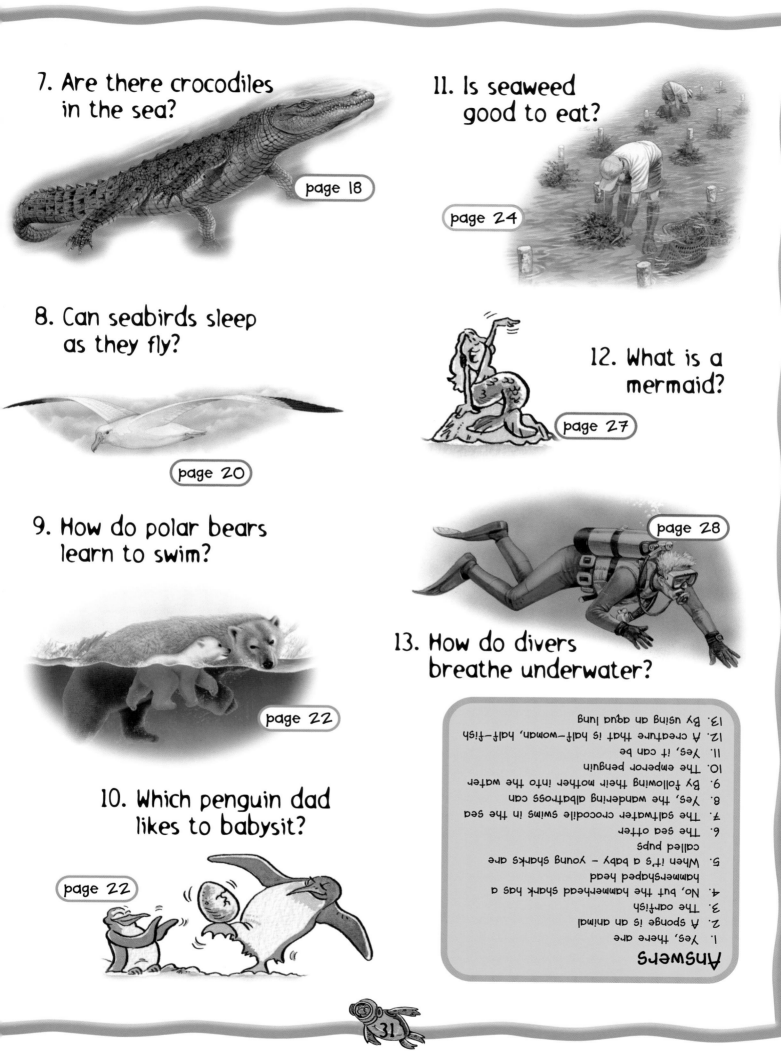

page 18

11. Is seaweed good to eat?

page 24

8. Can seabirds sleep as they fly?

page 20

12. What is a mermaid?

page 27

9. How do polar bears learn to swim?

page 28

page 22

13. How do divers breathe underwater?

10. Which penguin dad likes to babysit?

page 22

Answers

1. Yes, there are
2. A sponge is an animal
3. The oarfish
4. No, but the hammerhead shark has a hammershaped head
5. When it's a baby – young sharks are called pups
6. The sea otter
7. The saltwater crocodile swims in the sea
8. Yes, the wandering albatross can
9. By following their mother into the water
10. The emperor penguin
11. Yes, it can be
12. A creature that is half–woman, half–fish
13. By using an aqua lung

Index